To, Too, or Two?

Do you ever mix up the words *to, too,* and *two*? Study the words and what they mean. Then read the sentences and write the missing words.

---

to   means direction toward; also used before action words
The bus will take us **to** camp. I want **to** go.

too   means extreme or also
This road is **too** bumpy. I think so, **too**!

two   means the number 2
The bus ride takes **two** hours.

---

1. Jenny is going _____ camp next week.

2. Her twin sister, Jessica, is going, _____ .

3. The _____ girls will share a tent.

4. Jenny's friend Mae would like _____ go also.

5. But she will be _____ busy.

6. This summer Mae is helping her _____ cousins.

7. They rent bikes _____ people who are on vacation.

8. Mae is going to serve lemonade, _____ .

9. Her cousins will pay her _____ dollars a day.

There, Their, or They're?

Do you ever mix up the words *there, their,* and *they're*?
Study the words and what they mean.
Then read the sentences and write the missing words.

there	a place I have never been **there**.
their	belonging to them **Their** trip will last three weeks.
they're	they are **They're** having fun.

1. Dante and Tara are visiting _____ grandparents.

2. _____ grandparents live in Hawaii.

3. Dante and Tara have never been _____ .

4. _____ flying in an airplane.

5. They will get _____ in eight hours.

6. They will call their parents when they get _____ .

7. _____ home will be near the beach.

8. Dante and Tara want to spend a lot of time _____ .

9. _____ going to learn how to surf.

10. They will take lots of pictures on _____ trip.

Happy Birthday!

Read the story. Choose the correct word from the box to write on the blank.

year years

1. My best friend, Scott, is eight _____ old.

party parties

2. Today he is having a birthday _____ .

toy toys

3. I went to the store to buy him a _____ .

puzzle puzzles

4. I wanted to get him a dinosaur _____ .

animal animals

5. But then I saw the different sets of _____ .

whale whales

6. Scott likes _____ a lot.

gift gifts

7. I wrapped the two _____ .

hour hours

8. Now I'm ready to go. The party starts in just one more _____ .

FS-11054 Grammar Review Grade 2

A High-Wheeler Bike

Read the story. Then proofread it. Find and circle the nouns that are wrong. Write each correctly on the line. Use nouns from the bicycle.

bicycle
bicycles
parade
pedals
wheel
wheels

1. _____ My neighbor has an old bicycles.

2. _____ It has two wheel. But the wheels are

not the same size. The back wheel

3. _____ is little. The front wheels is very big.

I tried to climb on the bicycle. But

4. _____ the pedal were so high that I

couldn't. My neighbor can climb on it.

5. _____ He rode the bicycle in a parades last

week. When I get older, I think I will

6. _____ work with bicycle. I like them a lot.

Animal Actions

Action words that tell about one thing have an **s** added to the end.

Action words that tell about more than one thing do not have an **s** added.

*One kangaroo **jumps**.*

*Two kangaroos **jump**.*

Write the correct word from the box to finish each sentence.

play plays	1. One monkey _____ on the ropes. Four monkeys _____ on the ropes.
howl howls	2. One wolf _____ at the moon. Many wolves _____ at the moon.
eat eats	3. Birds _____ worms. A bird _____ worms.
run runs	4. Cheetahs _____ fast. The cheetah _____ fast.
live lives	5. A frog _____ in water and on land. Frogs _____ in water and on land.

Desert Life

A class is telling what they know about the desert. Choose action words from the cactus to fill in the blanks.

fall

falls

hunt

hunts

make

makes

grow

grows

sting

stings

find

finds

hop

hops

eat

eats

Only a little rain _____ in the desert.

Coyotes _____ for food at night.

Some owls _____ their home in a cactus.

Many different cactuses _____ in the desert.

A scorpion _____ with its tail.

A lizard _____ a shady place when it gets hot.

Jack rabbits _____ through the desert.

Some animals _____ cactus fruit.

FS-11054 Grammar Review Grade 2

Perky Isn't Perfect

Perky Parrot is learning to speak.
Perky needs your help using **am**, **is**, and **are**.
- Use **is** with one person, place, or thing.
- Use **are** with more than one or with the word *you*.
- Use **am** with the word *I*.

Read what Perky says. If the **boldfaced** word is correct, write *correct*. If the **boldfaced** word is wrong, circle it. Write the correct word on the line.

correct   I **am** a smart bird.

Are   (Is) you a smart bird?

_____ 1. You **are** my friend.

_____ 2. Most of my friends **is** birds.

_____ 3. But they **are** not talking birds.

_____ 4. They **is** very quiet birds.

_____ 5. My best friend **are** a bird named Wing.

_____ 6. I **is** in a cage.

_____ 7. Some birds **are** not in cages.

_____ 8. Some birds **is** outside.

A New Baby!

Read each sentence. Fill in the circle beside the verb that completes the sentence.

- Use **was** with one person, place, or thing.
- Use **were** with more than one or with the word *you*.

1. My little sister _____ born yesterday. ○ was ○ were	2. I _____ at the hospital. ○ was ○ were	3. My grandma and grandpa _____ staying with me. ○ was ○ were
4. My sister _____ sleepy. ○ was ○ were	5. Mom and Dad _____ sleepy, too. ○ was ○ were	6. Our baby _____ quiet. ○ was ○ were
7. All the other babies _____ crying. ○ was ○ were	8. We _____ all so happy to have a new baby. ○ was ○ were	9. Yesterday _____ a great day! ○ was ○ were

FS-11054 Grammar Review Grade 2

When I Was Young

Write the correct verb from
the box to finish this poem.

talk
talked

When I was young, I never _____ .

Now I _____ all day.

walked
walk

When I was young, I never _____ .

Now I _____ all day.

slept
sleep

When I was young, I _____ all day.

Now I _____ a little.

creep
crept

When I was young, I _____ all day.

Now I _____ a little.

cry
cried

When I was young, I _____ a lot.

Now I hardly _____ .

tried
try

When I was young, I _____ a lot.

Even now I _____ .

That's Not a Word!

Read each sentence. Fill in the circle beside the past tense verb that completes the sentence.

1. Yesterday I ____ to the fair with my family. ○ goed ○ went	2. We ____ a lot of things. ○ doed ○ did	3. First, we ____ at animals. ○ looked ○ lookt
4. I ____ the biggest cow in the world! ○ seed ○ saw	5. Next, we ____ on some rides. ○ goed ○ went	6. My brother ____ the Ferris wheel was his favorite. ○ sayed ○ said
7. I ____ the roller coaster. ○ liked ○ likt		8. Then we ____ lunch. ○ eated ○ ate
9. I ____ three slices of pizza. ○ haved ○ had	10. Later we ____ games. ○ played ○ playd	11. I ____ a toy dinosaur. ○ winned ○ won

FS-11054 Grammar Review Grade 2

Favorite Birthdays

The verbs in these stories should all be in the past tense. Read each story. Find and circle the verb that is wrong. Write the sentence correctly.

My favorite birthday was when I turned six. I (get) to take the braces off my legs. It felt great to walk without them.

I got to take the braces off my legs.

My favorite birthday was when I turned five. My dad dress up like a clown. He made balloon animals for us.

_____

_____

Last year was my favorite birthday. My cousins came over. We act out plays for everyone.

_____

_____

Story Time

Read these stories. Choose the correct verb from the box. Write it on the line. Keep all the actions in the past or all in the present.

| is was |

1.   Once upon a time a rude princess lived in a castle. She _____ not very nice. She never said "Please" or "Thank you."

| jumps jumped |

2.   I love my cat Zigzag. He does funny things. He runs a little this way. Then he runs a little that way. Then he _____ on a chair.

| looks looked |

3.   The Tyrannosaurus Rex _____ around. It opened its mouth and let out a roar. The plant-eating dinosaurs were scared.

| play played |

4.   Tonight is Game Night at our school. Families come and _____ math games together. There are even games for very young children.

| stops stopped |

5.   Last week I rode on a subway. The subway train _____ at our station. The doors opened. We climbed inside. It was crowded so we had to stand.

Sea Otters

Read the sentences. Choose the pronoun from the clam that matches the **boldfaced** subject. Write it on the line.

They / We

1. **My class and I** are learning about sea otters.

   _____ are learning about sea otters.

He / It

2. **Nick** has a picture of a sea otter.

   _____ has a picture of a sea otter.

He / It

3. **The picture** shows the sea otter on its back.

   _____ shows the sea otter on its back.

They / We

4. **Sea otters** eat clams and other shellfish.

   _____ eat clams and other shellfish.

We / It

5. **A sea otter** uses the rock to crack open a clam.

   _____ uses the rock to crack open a clam.

We / They

6. **Robin and I** are writing riddles about sea otters.

   _____ are writing riddles about sea otters.

Little Bo-Peep

Read the nursery rhyme. Look at the pronouns that take the place of Bo-Peep's sheep. Then read the other rhymes. Write the missing pronouns on the lines. Use words from the sheep.

me us
her you
them

Little Bo-Peep has lost <u>her sheep</u>
And doesn't know where to find <u>them</u>.
Leave <u>them</u> alone and they'll come home
Wagging their tails behind <u>them</u>.

Cory and Matt have lost <u>their cat</u>

And don't know where to find _____ .

Leave _____ alone and she'll come home

Wagging her tail behind _____ .

Farmer McVie has lost <u>you and me</u>

And doesn't know where to find _____ .

Leave _____ alone and we'll come home

Pulling our wagon behind _____ .

Bluebird Boxes

Read the story. The **boldfaced** words are mistakes. Write the correct pronoun on the line. Use words from the bluebird box.

Our science club is doing a bluebird

1. _____ project. **Us** are making bluebird boxes.

2. _____ Carmen's dad is helping us. **Him** shows us

how to nail the wood pieces together.

We will put the boxes in the park.

Bluebirds make their nests in tree holes.

3. _____ But there aren't enough tree holes for **they**.

4. _____ Now **them** can build nests in our boxes.

5. _____ My friends and **me** will check the boxes

each week. We want to see if any

6. _____ bluebirds are using **it**. We will look for

nests, eggs, and chicks.

Wish You Were Here!

Read the postcards. Write the missing pronouns.

1. Use **they**, **us**, or **we**.

> Dear Class,
>
> My family and I went to a museum today.
>
> _____ had a good time. A man showed
>
> _____ Navajo blankets and jewelry.
>
> > Your friend,
> > Alex

2. Use **I**, **it**, or **you**.

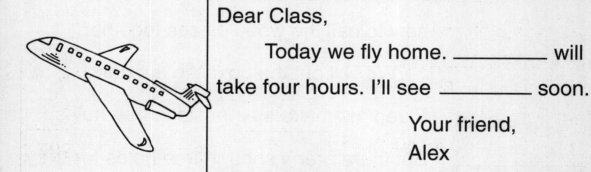

> Dear Class,
>
> Today we fly home. _____ will
>
> take four hours. I'll see _____ soon.
>
> > Your friend,
> > Alex

3. Use **I**, **he**, or **him**.

> Dear Class,
>
> Today _____ went to a fort. My
>
> brother was with me. _____ got lost.
>
> > Your friend,
> > Alex

 FS-11054 Grammar Review Grade 2

My Friends and I

When you talk or write about someone
else and yourself, name yourself last.

Lynn and I are friends.
Jeff rides bikes with Karen and me.

Read the sentences. Write them correctly.

1. **I and John** like to swim.

_____

2. Erika hikes with **me and Steve**.

_____

3. **I and Kevin** read comic books.

_____

4. Ann draws **me and my fish**.

_____

5. Pete skates with **me and Tom**.

_____

6. **I and Marta** play the piano.

_____

For the Birds

Melinda's class is studying birds.
She made a list of birds she has never seen.
Complete the list by adding **a** or **an** before each bird.

- Use **an** if the next word starts with a vowel sound.
- Use **a** if the next word starts with a consonant sound.

Examples: **an** animal   **a** bird

1. _____ pelican

2. _____ ibis

3. _____ toucan

4. _____ dodo

5. _____ albatross

6. _____ loon

7. _____ owl

8. _____ egret

9. _____ condor

10. _____ umbrella bird

11. _____ nene

12. _____ osprey

13. _____ quetzal

14. _____ kookaburra

15. _____ auk

16. _____ puffin

17. _____ ostrich

18. _____ emu

19. _____ vulture

20. _____ lovebird

FS-11054 Grammar Review Grade 2

Helicopters

Every sentence begins with a capital letter. Read the story. Circle each letter that should be a capital. Write the word correctly on the line.

1. _____   do you know what a chopper

2. _____   is? a chopper is another word for

3. _____   a helicopter. a helicopter is a flying

4. _____   machine. it can fly up, down,

frontwards, backwards, and

5. _____   sideways! it can also stay right

6. _____   where it is in the air. that is called

7. _____   hovering. some helicopters are

8. _____   small. they can only carry one

9. _____   person. other helicopters are very

10. _____   big. they can carry lots of people

or even trucks.

     FS-11054 Grammar Review Grade 2

My New Glasses

Every sentence begins with a capital letter. Read the story. Circle each letter that should be a capital. Write the story correctly.

i went to the eye doctor. she had me read rows of letters. my doctor said I needed glasses. i got to pick the frames. now I can see clearly!

Who Likes to Do It?

Names always begin with a capital letter. The word **I** does, too.
Sarah, Ron, and I like to tell stories.
Finish the sentences by writing names of people you know.

1. _____ likes to read books.

2. _____ thinks of good ideas.

3. _____ likes math.

4. _____ and _____ run fast.

5. _____ likes to draw.

6. _____ makes things.

7. _____ likes to do puzzles.

8. _____ writes well.

9. _____ likes to sing.

FS-11054 Grammar Review Grade 2

Holiday Fun

Write each sentence correctly. Remember to begin months of the year and names of holidays with a capital letter.

1. january 1 is new year's day.

2. easter is in march or april.

3. mother's day is in may.

4. father's day is in june.

5. october 31 is halloween.

6. thanksgiving is in november.

FS-11054 Grammar Review Grade 2

Christopher Columbus

Proofread the story. Dates and names of special people, places, and things should begin with capital letters. Circle the words that need a capital letter. Write them correctly on the lines.

Columbus

1. _____

2. _____

3. _____

4. _____

5. _____

6. _____

7. _____

8. _____

9. _____

Christopher (columbus) was a famous explorer. He sailed west from spain across the atlantic Ocean. His three ships were named the Pinta, the niña, and the santa Maria. Columbus was trying to find the Indies.

On october 12, 1492, columbus landed on an island. Because he thought he had found the indies, he called the people he saw indians. But Columbus had not found the Indies. He had sailed to america.

Names and Initials

An initial is the first letter of a name or word. It is written as a capital letter followed by a period. Read the list of names. Write the initials.

Writing Club

Name (First	Middle	Last)	Initials
1. Sean	Daniel	McDowell	S.D.M.
2. Kim	April	Davis	_____
3. Michael	Alan	Wong	_____
4. Grace	Ellen	Varani	_____
5. Brian	Jamal	Reed	_____
6. Eva	Maria	Lopez	_____
7. Amber	Lee	Brown	_____
8. Justin	James	Fox	_____
9. Ebony	Nicole	Smith	_____
10. Aaron	Amit	Cooper	_____
11. Hector	Ramon	Trujillo	_____
12. Claire	Renee	Salem	_____

FS-11054 Grammar Review Grade 2

Favorite Books

What are your favorite books? Write their titles below. Begin the first, the last, and each important word in a title with a capital letter.

Picture Books

A Chair for My Mother

_____

_____

Folk Tales

Tikki Tikki Tembo

_____

_____

Informational Books

My Visit to the Dinosaurs

_____

_____

Dear Pen Pal

In a friendly letter these words begin with a capital letter:
- the date
- the first word in the greeting
- the first word in the closing
- the first word in each sentence
- special names of people, places, or things
- the word I

Date	April 5, 1997
Greeting	Dear Pen Pal,
Body	My name is Chris. I like music, science, and P.E. I have two dogs.
Closing	Your new friend,
Signature	Chris

Read this letter. Circle the seven words that should begin with a capital letter.

april 19, 1997

dear Chris,

My name is terry. I like music, too. I also like math and reading.

I don't have any pets. I wish i did. I do have a sister and a brother. my parents say that with three kids, they don't need any pets.

My grandparents are deaf. I use sign language to talk to them. do you know any sign language?

your friend,

Terry

Pull-Out Answers

Page 1
1. to   4. to   7. to
2. too   5. too   8. too
3. two   6. two   9. two

Page 2
1. their   6. there
2. Their   7. Their
3. there   8. there
4. They're   9. They're
5. there   10. their

Page 3
1. years   5. animals
2. party   6. whales
3. toy   7. gifts
4. puzzle   8. hour

Page 4
Words that should be circled
are boldfaced below.
1. bicycle   **bicycles**
2. wheels   **wheel**
3. wheel   **wheels**
4. pedals   **pedal**
5. parade   **parades**
6. bicycles   **bicycle**

Page 5
1. plays   4. run
   play   runs
2. howls   5. lives
   howl   live
3. eat
   eats

Page 6
Only a little rain <u>falls</u> . . .
Coyotes <u>hunt</u> for food at night.
Some owls <u>make</u> their . . .
Many different cactuses <u>grow</u> . . .
A scorpion <u>stings</u> with its tail.
A lizard <u>finds</u> a shady place . . .
Jack rabbits <u>hop</u> through . . .
Some animals <u>eat</u> cactus fruit.

Page 7
1. correct   5. is
2. are   6. am
3. correct   7. correct
4. are   8. are

Page 8
1. was   2. was   3. were
4. was   5. were   6. was
7. were   8. were   9. was

Page 9
talked   walked
talk   walk
slept   crept
sleep   creep
cried   tried
cry   try

Page 10
1. went   2. did   3. looked
4. saw   5. went   6. said
7. liked   8. ate   9. had
10. played   11. won

Page 11
(dress)
My dad dressed up like a clown.
(act)
We acted out plays for everyone.

Page 12
1. was   4. play
2. jumps   5. stopped
3. looked

Page 13
1. We   3. It   5. It
2. He   4. They   6. We

Page 14
<u>her</u>   <u>us</u>
<u>her</u>   <u>us</u>
<u>her</u>   <u>us</u>

Page 15
1. We   3. them   5. I
2. He   4. they   6. them

Page 16
1. We   2. It   3. I
   us   you   He/I

Page 17
1. John and I like to swim.
2. Erika hikes with Steve and me.
3. Kevin and I read comic books.
4. Ann draws my fish and me.
5. Pete skates with Tom and me.
6. Marta and I play the piano.

Page 18
1. a   6. a   11. a   16. a
2. an   7. an   12. an   17. an
3. a   8. an   13. a   18. an
4. a   9. a   14. a   19. a
5. an   10. an   15. an   20. a

Page 19
Words that should be circled
are boldfaced below.
1. Do   **do**
2. A   **a**
3. A   **a**
4. It   **it**
5. It   **it**
6. That   **that**
7. Some   **some**
8. They   **they**
9. Other   **other**
10. They   **they**

Page 20
Words that should be circled:
   i   she   my   i   now

A

Pull-Out Answers

Page 21
Answers will vary but should begin with capital letters.

Page 22
1. January 1 is New Year's Day.
2. Easter is in March or April.
3. Mother's Day is in May.
4. Father's Day is in June.
5. October 31 is Halloween.
6. Thanksgiving is in November.

Page 23
Words that should be circled are boldfaced below.
1. Spain **spain**
2. Atlantic **atlantic**
3. Niña **niña**
4. Santa **santa**
5. October **october**
6. Columbus **columbus**
7. Indies **indies**
8. Indians **indians**
9. America **america**

Page 24
1. S.D.M.
2. K.A.D.
3. M.A.W.
4. G.E.V.
5. B.J.R.
6. E.M.L.
7. A.L.B.
8. J.J.F.
9. E.N.S.
10. A.A.C.
11. H.R.T.
12. C.R.S.

Page 25
Answers will vary but should be titles.

Page 26
Words that should be circled:
april   dear   terry   i
my   do   your

Page 27
Words that should be circled are boldfaced below.
1. June **june**
2. Dear **dear**
3. It **it**
4. Sky **sky**
5. July **july**
6. I **i**
7. My **my**
8. Madison **madison**
9. Your **your**
10. Kelly **kelly**

Page 28
Sierra: We could grow different kinds of seeds.

Joe: Yeah. We could see which kind grows fastest.

Ann: Do we have to buy the seeds?

Devin: Ms. Walsh has seeds we can use.

Sierra: Which kinds does she have?

Devin: I'll go check.

Joe: How many different kinds should we plant?

Ann: Let's plant a whole bunch.

Joe: Do you each want to pick one kind?

Sierra: O.K. I pick carrots.

Devin: I'll choose peas.

Joe: I pick beans.

Ann: I want to plant lettuce.

Sierra: Let's write our plan.

Page 29
Have you ever played with shadows? It is fun to play with shadows.

You can play outside on a sunny day. Do you know how to play shadow tag? One person is It. That person tries to tag the other players' shadows.

Do you think your shadow is always the same length? Look at it in the morning. Look at it at noon. Then look at it late in the day. When is it longest? When is it shortest?

You can also play with shadows indoors. It is more fun if you do it with a friend or someone in your family. Start with a dark room. Shine a bright flashlight on a wall. Make shapes with your hands. Put them between the light and the wall. What do you see on the wall?

Page 30
Zonk: We better land on Earth.
Zink: Good idea! or .
Zonk: Yikes, what a bumpy landing!
Zink: Let's look around.
Zonk: Have you ever been to Earth?
Zink: No. Have you?
Zonk: No. My mother came here once.
Zink: What did she say about it?
Zonk: She said Earthlings look weird but most are nice.
Zink: I see Earthlings coming now. Hide!
Zonk: They're moving very fast.
Zink: Look! They have wheels for feet!

Pull-Out Answers

Page 31

Last night my parents told me I had to clean my room. I looked around. What a mess! Then I fell asleep.

I dreamed a monster came. Do you know what it did? It did whatever I asked. So I told the monster to put away all my clothes. It hung them up nicely. Then I told it to put all my books back on the shelves. It did. Next, I told the monster to clean up my toys. The monster did that, too. It was great! My room was clean and I didn't do any of the work.

Then I woke up. My room was still a mess. The monster hadn't really come. I guess I better start cleaning.

Page 32

February — Dec.
April — Sept.
December — Feb.
September — Apr.
August — Nov.
November — Aug.
January — Tues.
March — Mar.
Tuesday — Jan.
Monday — Wed.
Wednesday — Fri.
Friday — Mon.
October — Sat.
Saturday — Oct.

Page 33

1. What's going on?
2. Who's making all that . . .
3. We're a marching band!
4. You're too noisy.
5. I can't do my homework.
6. We didn't mean to . . .
7. Let's go bother Mom!

Page 34

Words that should be circled are boldfaced below.

1. They're **Theyre**
2. I'm **Im**
3. That's **Thats**
4. She's **Shes**
5. It's **Its**
6. don't **dont**
7. There's **Theres**

Page 35

Deb	January 2, 1988
Mom	February 26, 1962
Brad	March 13, 1994
Grandpa	April 1, 1931
Ricky	May 8, 1992
Dad	June 30, 1963
Aunt Valerie	July 4, 1964
Damon	August 14, 1992
Danielle	August 14, 1992
Curtis	September 5, 1995
Gran	October 31, 1940
Granddad	December 9, 1938

Page 36

1. Pablo Picasso was born October 25, 1881.
2. Georgia O'Keeffe was born November 15, 1887.
3. Vincent van Gogh was born March 30, 1853.
4. Claude Monet was born November 14, 1840.

Page 37

August 9, 1997

Dear Tony,

I like my new house. There is a nice girl next door. She has a tree house. But I miss my friends at the trailer park.

Your friend,
Robbie

September 3, 1997

Dear Robbie,

School started yesterday. It was weird to walk to school without you. How is your new school?

Your friend,
Tony

Page 38

May 5, 1997

Dear Miss Robles,

Thank you for showing us around the museum. We liked learning about the Aztecs. Our favorite part was finding out what games Aztec children played. How do you know so much about the Aztecs?

We made a big drawing when we got back to school. It shows all the different things we learned. Would you like to visit our school and see it?

Thank you again for our fun trip.

Sincerely,
Miss Schell's Class

Page 39

I like horses. Last week I got to ride one for the first time. I want to go riding again.

Pull-Out Answers

Page 40
Answers will vary.

Page 41
1. Do   3. I
2. We   4. August

(do) you have . . . park? Our school playground has . . . and slides. But the . . . is old. Some of . . . broken. So we are getting a new playground.

The children . . . plan it. (we) write our . . we want. Do you . . . idea is? (i) want . . .swing.

We are hoping . . . in June. Then it . . . starts in (august.)

Page 42
What is your favorite flower? I love tulips. Last year (i) planted some in our yard.

In the fall . . . my parents. (we) bought bulbs. Have you . . . a tulip bulb? It looks . . . a ball.

We dug . . . the soil. I put . . . each hole. (next,) I . . . with soil. The bulbs . . . during winter.

Then in (march) the . . . from the bulbs. There were tulips everywhere. It was lovely!

Page 43
1. blueberry   2. goldfish
3. greenhouse 4. blackboard
5. redwood   6. silverfish
7. blackbird   8. bluebell

Page 44
1. <u>walk</u>   <u>across</u> crosswalk
2. <u>sun</u>   <u>burn</u> sunburn
3. <u>spread</u> <u>bed</u> bedspread
4. <u>wear</u>   <u>under</u> underwear
5. <u>scare</u>   <u>crow</u> scarecrow
6. <u>snake</u>   <u>rattle</u> rattlesnake

Page 44 cont.
7. <u>tack</u>   <u>thumb</u> thumbtack
8. <u>corn</u>   <u>pop</u> popcorn
9. <u>ball</u>   <u>basket</u> basketball
10. <u>door</u>   <u>bell</u> doorbell
11. <u>wood</u>   <u>fire</u> firewood

Page 45
1. can't   2. I'm   3. he's
4. you've 5. doesn't 6. she'll
7. they're 8. isn't   9. that's

Page 46

I have — I'm
I would — I've
I am — I'll
I will — I'd

you will — you'll
you would — you're
you have — you'd
you are — you've

can not — couldn't
could not — can't
do not — didn't
did not — don't
will not — won't
was not — wasn't

who is — what'll
what will — what's
who would — who's
what is — who'd

Page 47
1. world   5. try
2. find   6. largest
3. lowest   7. country
4. blue-green 8. people

Page 48
Answers will vary. Accept reasonable answers.

Page 49

make — lose
stop — destroy
find — dislike
like — start
work — cool
cry — play
push — pull
heat — laugh

first — bad
asleep — sad
good — last
happy — awake
hard — soft
shiny — her
many — dull
his — cruel
left — short
kind — few
fancy — right
tall — plain

quietly — clumsily
gracefully — quickly
happily — loudly
slowly — sadly

Page 50
1. new   4. two   6. our
2. I   5. too   7. no
3. won

Page 51
1. uneven   3. unhappy
2. unkind   4. unsafe

Page 52
1. painful   2. careful
3. joyful   4. playful
5. colorful   6. hopeful
7. powerful   8. thoughtful

A Friendly Letter

Read this letter. Circle the 10 words that should begin with a capital letter. Write them correctly on the lines.

1. _____

2. _____

3. _____

4. _____

5. _____

6. _____

7. _____

8. _____

9. _____

10. _____

june 21, 1997

dear Shane,

   Thank you for the postcard you sent. it sounds like you are having fun at Big sky Camp.

   My birthday is july 10. My parents said i could invite one friend to go to a movie. Would you please come?

   my sister cut her hand yesterday. We had to take her to madison Community Hospital for stitches.

   I'll see you soon.

your friend,

kelly

27

A Plant Experiment

Four children are planning an experiment.
Read their conversation.
Write a period (.) at the end of telling sentences.
Write a question mark (?) at the end of asking sentences.

Ann: We need to do a seed experiment.

Devin: Do you have any ideas?

Sierra: We could grow different kinds of seeds

Joe: Yeah. We could see which kind grows fastest

Ann: Do we have to buy the seeds

Devin: Ms. Walsh has seeds we can use

Sierra: Which kinds does she have

Devin: I'll go check

Joe: How many different kinds should we plant

Ann: Let's plant a whole bunch

Joe: Do you each want to pick one kind

Sierra: O.K. I pick carrots

Devin: I'll choose peas

Joe: I pick beans

Ann: I want to plant lettuce

Sierra: Let's write our plan

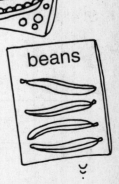

Shadow Fun

Read this story. Write the missing punctuation.
Telling sentences end with a period. (.)
Asking sentences end with a question mark. (?)

Have you ever played with shadows   It is fun to
play with shadows

You can play outside on a sunny day   Do you
know how to play shadow tag   One person is It
That person tries to tag the other players' shadows

Do you think your shadow is always the same
length   Look at it in the morning   Look at it at noon
Then look at it late in the day   When is it longest
When is it shortest

You can also play with shadows indoors   It is
more fun if you do it with a friend or someone in
your family   Start with a dark room   Shine a bright
flashlight on a wall   Make shapes with your hands
Put them between the light and the wall   What do
you see on the wall

Zink and Zonk

Zink and Zonk are aliens. Read their conversation.
Write a period (**.**) at the end of telling sentences.
Write a question mark (**?**) at the end of asking sentences.
Write an exclamation mark (**!**) at the end of sentences that show strong feelings.

Zink: Oh, no **!**

Zonk: What's wrong **?**

Zink: Our spaceship is low on fuel **.**

Zonk: We better land on Earth

Zink: Good idea

Zonk: Yikes, what a bumpy landing

Zink: Let's look around

Zonk: Have you ever been to Earth

Zink: No. Have you

Zonk: No. My mother came here once

Zink: What did she say about it

Zonk: She said Earthlings look weird but most are nice

Zink: I see Earthlings coming now. Hide

Zonk: They're moving very fast

Zink: Look! They have wheels for feet

What a Mess!

Read this story. Write the missing punctuation.
Telling sentences end with a period. (**.**)
Asking sentences end with a question mark. (**?**)
Sentences that show strong feelings end with
an exclamation mark. (**!**)

Last night my parents told me I had to clean my room   I
looked around   What a mess   Then I fell asleep

I dreamed a monster came   Do you know what it did   It
did whatever I asked   So I told the monster to put away all my
clothes   It hung them up nicely   Then I told it to put all my
books back on the shelves   It did   Next, I told the monster to
clean up my toys   The monster did that, too   It was great
My room was clean and I didn't do any of the work

Then I woke up   My room was still a mess   The monster
hadn't really come   I guess I better
start cleaning

31

Abbreviation Match-up

Match each month or day of the week to its abbreviation.
Write a period at the end of the abbreviation to finish it.

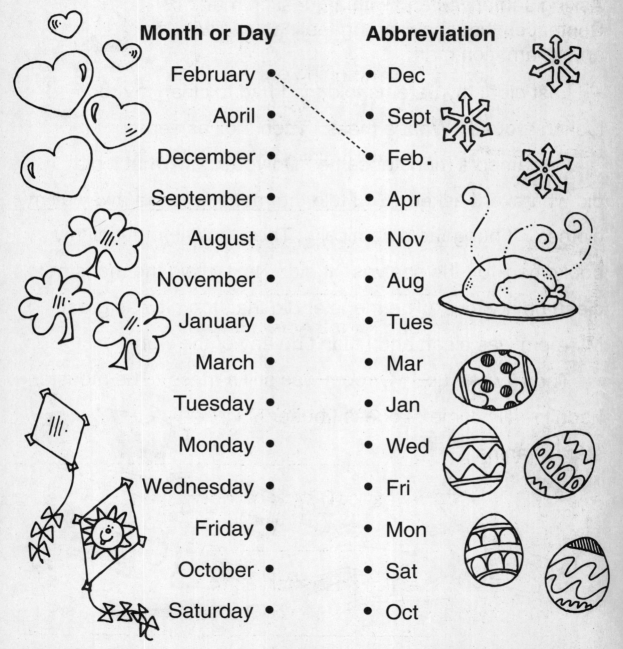

Month or Day		Abbreviation
February •	•	Dec
April •	•	Sept
December •	•	Feb.
September •	•	Apr
August •	•	Nov
November •	•	Aug
January •	•	Tues
March •	•	Mar
Tuesday •	•	Jan
Monday •	•	Wed
Wednesday •	•	Fri
Friday •	•	Mon
October •	•	Sat
Saturday •	•	Oct

A Marching Band

Rewrite each sentence. Change the
words in parentheses to a contraction.
Take out the **boldfaced** letters.
Put in an apostrophe (').

1. (What **is**) going on?

   <u>What's going on?</u>

2. (Who **is**) making all that noise?

   _____

3. (We **a**re) a marching band!

   _____

4. (You **a**re) too noisy.

   _____

5. I (can **no**t) do my homework.

   _____

6. We (did n**o**t) mean to bother you.

   _____

7. (Let **u**s) go bother Mom!

   _____

Two Families

The contractions in the story below
are missing the apostrophes (').
Find and circle the contractions.
Write them correctly on the lines.

1. They're

2. _____

3. _____

4. _____

5. _____

6. _____

7. _____

I have two families. (Theyre) in different cities.

During the school year I live with my mom and my brother. Im older than my brother. Thats why I have to do most of the chores.

I also have a sister. Shes just a baby. She lives with my dad and my stepmom. My brother and I live with them in the summer. Its crowded with three kids. But we dont mind. Theres always something going on.

Birthday List

Deb made a list of birthdays. She forgot to write a comma (,) between each day and year. Write the missing commas. Then finish the list with your name and birthday.

Name	Birthday
Deb	January 2, 1988
Mom	February 26 1962
Brad	March 13 1994
Grandpa	April 1 1931
Ricky	May 8 1992
Dad	June 30 1963
Aunt Valerie	July 4 1964
Damon	August 14 1992
Danielle	August 14 1992
Curtis	September 5 1995
Gran	October 31 1940
Granddad	December 9 1938

_____   _____

Famous Artists' Birthdays

Read the chart. Write sentences to answer the questions.
Remember to write a comma (,) between the day and year.
Example: Diego Rivera was born December 8, 1886.

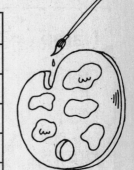

Artist	Month	Day	Year
Claude Monet	November	14	1840
Grandma Moses	September	7	1860
Georgia O'Keeffe	November	15	1887
Pablo Picasso	October	25	1881
Diego Rivera	December	8	1886
Vincent van Gogh	March	30	1853

1. When was Pablo Picasso born?

_____

2. When was Georgia O'Keeffe born?

_____

3. When was Vincent van Gogh born?

_____

4. When was Claude Monet born?

_____

Missing Commas

In a friendly letter use a comma (,) in these places:
- between the day and year in the date
- at the end of the greeting
- at the end of the closing

Date	July 21, 1997
Greeting	Dear Robbie,
Body	How do you like your new house? Have you made any friends yet? Write back!
Closing	Your friend,
Signature	Tony

Read these letters. Write the missing commas.

August 9 1997

Dear Tony
    I like my new house. There is a nice girl next door. She has a tree house. But I miss my friends at the trailer park.
        Your friend
        Robbie

September 3 1997

Dear Robbie
    School started yesterday. It was weird to walk to school without you. How is your new school?
        Your friend
        Tony

Oops! No Punctuation

Find and write the missing punctuation marks in this letter.
Check off (✔) each box after you find the missing marks.

☐ 3 commas (,)

☐ 2 question marks (?)

☐ 6 periods (.)

May 5   1997

Dear Miss Robles

Thank you for showing us around the museum   We liked learning about the Aztecs   Our favorite part was finding out what games Aztec children played   How do you know so much about the Aztecs

We made a big drawing when we got back to school   It shows all the different things we learned Would you like to visit our school and see it

Thank you again for our fun trip

Sincerely

Miss Schell's Class

Writing Paragraphs

A paragraph is a group of sentences written about the same idea. To show a paragraph is starting, you **indent**, or move in, the first sentence.

Sentences	Paragraph
1. I have a new puppy. 2. My puppy sleeps a lot. 3. I love my puppy!	I have a new puppy. My puppy sleeps a lot. I love my puppy!

Read these sentences. Write them as a paragraph.

Sentences
1. I like horses.
2. Last week I got to ride one for the first time.
3. I want to go riding again.

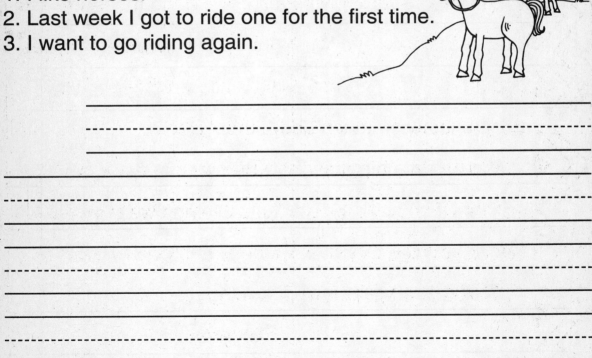

Animal Paragraphs

List three facts you know about an animal. Then write the facts as a paragraph. Remember to indent the first sentence.

Facts
1. Hedgehogs are small animals.
2. They have spines on their backs.
3. Hedgehogs curl up in a ball if they get scared.

Paragraph
   Hedgehogs are small animals. They have spines on their backs. Hedgehogs curl up in a ball if they get scared.

1. _____

2. _____

3. _____

_____

_____

_____

_____

The New Playground

Proofread this story. Check off (✔) each step as you do it.

☐ Circle the 4 words that should begin with a capital letter. Write them correctly on the lines.

☐ Write the 2 missing question marks.

☐ Write the 4 missing periods.

1. _____   do you have a playground at your

school or park Our school playground

has swings, bars, and slides. But the

equipment is old Some of it is broken.

So we are getting a new playground

The children get to help plan it.

2. _____ we write our ideas and draw pictures

of what we want Do you know what

3. _____ my idea is i want a tire swing.

We are hoping to start work on

the playground in June Then it will be

4. _____ ready when school starts in august.

Tulip Time

Proofread this story. Check off (✔) each step as you do it.

☐ Circle the 4 words that should begin with a capital letter.

☐ Write the 2 missing question marks.

☐ Write the 4 missing periods.

What is your favorite flower I love tulips. Last year i planted some in our yard

In the fall I went to a garden store with my parents. we bought bulbs Have you ever seen a tulip bulb It looks kind of like a ball.

We dug holes in the soil I put about six tulip bulbs in each hole. next, I covered them with soil. The bulbs just stayed underground during winter.

Then in march the tulips started to grow up from the bulbs. There were tulips everywhere It was lovely!

Colorful Compounds

Put the two words together to write a compound word.
Color the pictures to match.

1. blue + berry

_____

- - - - - - - - - - - - - - - - - - -

2. gold + fish

_____

- - - - - - - - - - - - - - - - - - -

3. green + house

_____

- - - - - - - - - - - - - - - - - - -

4. black + board

_____

- - - - - - - - - - - - - - - - - - -

5. red + wood

_____

- - - - - - - - - - - - - - - - - - -

6. silver + fish

_____

- - - - - - - - - - - - - - - - - - -

7. black + bird

_____

- - - - - - - - - - - - - - - - - - -

8. blue + bell

_____

- - - - - - - - - - - - - - - - - - -

Hidden Compounds

Read each sentence. Find and underline two words that make a compound word. Write the compound word.

basketball   bedspread   ◆   crosswalk   doorbell

popcorn   rattlesnake   scarecrow   firewood

sunburn   thumbtack   ◆   underwear

1. Let's <u>walk</u> <u>across</u> here. _____crosswalk_____

2. The sun is burning my skin. _____

3. I spread the cover over my bed. _____

4. I wear these under my clothes. _____

5. I hope this will scare the crows. _____

6. The snake rattles its tail to warn you. _____

7. Push in the tack with your thumb. _____

8. When it gets hot, the corn pops up. _____

9. Throw the ball through the basket! _____

10. I opened the door when I heard the bell. _____

11. Please bring in some wood for the fire. _____

Smooth Sailing

Write the contraction for each pair of words. Take out the underlined letters. Write an apostrophe (') in their place.

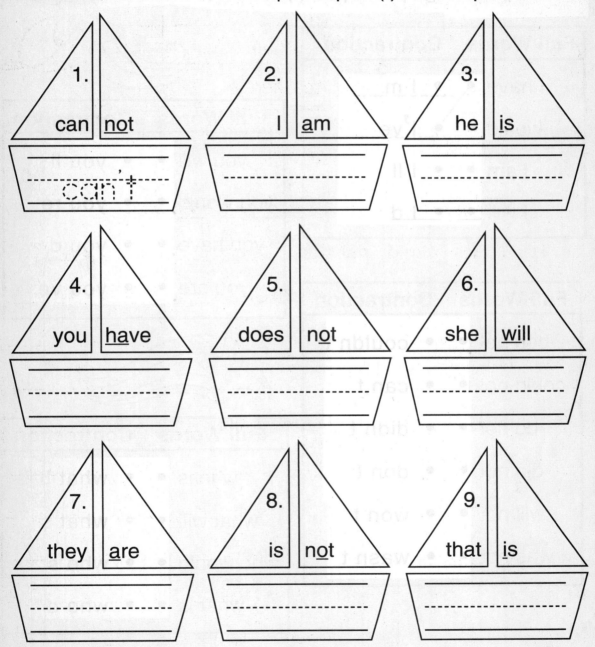

1. can not
   can't

2. I am

3. he is

4. you have

5. does not

6. she will

7. they are

8. is not

9. that is

Contraction Match-up

Write the contraction for these words.

Full Words	Contraction
I have	
I would	
I am	
I will	

Full Words	Contraction
you will	
you would	
you have	
you are	

Full Words	Contraction
can not	
could not	
do not	
did not	
will not	
was not	

Full Words	Contraction
who is	
what will	
who would	
what is	

FS-11054 Grammar Review Grade 2

Working With Globes

Fill in the circle next to the word that means about the same as the **boldfaced** word.

1. A globe is a round map of the **earth**. ○ world ○ school	2. Can you **locate** Antarctica? ○ take ○ find	3. It is at the **bottom** part of the globe. ○ lowest ○ newest
4. On some globes the water is a **turquoise** color. ○ wet ○ blue-green	5. Let's **attempt** to find our country on the globe. ○ give ○ try	6. Asia is the **biggest** continent. ○ largest ○ oldest
7. Canada is one **nation** you can see on a globe. ○ country ○ child	8. More **humans** live in China than in any other country. ○ fish ○ people	

Means the Same

For each word, write another word that has about the same meaning.

Nouns

1. insect _____
2. child _____
3. bunny _____
4. tale _____
5. pal _____
6. auto _____
7. drawing _____

Verbs

8. begin _____
9. yell _____
10. close _____
11. question _____
12. build _____
13. grab _____
14. sketch _____

Adjectives

15. beautiful _____
16. large _____
17. kind _____
18. many _____
19. frightening _____
20. noisy _____

FS-11054 Grammar Review Grade 2

Word Opposites

Draw lines to match each word to its opposite.

Verbs

make •	• lose
stop •	• destroy
find •	• dislike
like •	• start
work •	• cool
cry •	• play
push •	• pull
heat •	• laugh

Adverbs

quietly •	• clumsily
gracefully •	• quickly
happily •	• loudly
slowly •	• sadly

Adjectives

first •	• bad
asleep •	• sad
good •	• last
happy •	• awake
hard •	• soft
shiny •	• her
many •	• dull
his •	• cruel
left •	• short
kind •	• few
fancy •	• right
tall •	• plain

Sounds the Same

Fill in the circle beside the correct word for each sentence.

1. I have a _____ game.
   - ○ knew
   - ○ new

2. My friend and _____ played it.
   - ○ eye
   - ○ I

3. I _____ the first game.
   - ○ one
   - ○ won

4. My friend won the next _____ games.
   - ○ two
   - ○ too

5. My cat wanted to play, _____ .
   - ○ two
   - ○ too

6. She knocked over all _____ pieces.
   - ○ hour
   - ○ our

7. "Oh, _____ !" we yelled.
   - ○ know
   - ○ no

"Un" Words

The prefix *un* means "not." Write a new word by adding *un* to the beginning of each word. Draw a picture to match.

1. even    *uneven*

2. kind    _____

3. happy    _____

4. safe    _____

Full of . . .

The suffix *ful* means "full of." Change each word to an adjective by adding the suffix *ful*.

1. pain ___painful___

2. care _____

3. joy _____

4. play _____

5. color _____

6. hope _____

7. power _____

8. thought _____

     FS-11054 Grammar Review Grade 2